MW01528859

My Fir$t Million

Essential Money Tips from One of the World's Youngest Self-Made Millionaires

JAMES WHITE

BEAUFORT
BOOKS

MY FIRST MILLION
by James White

BEAUFORT
BOOKS

Beaufort Books, Inc.
27 West 20th St.
New York, NY 10011
(212) 727-0190
(212) 727-0195 fax
www.beaufortbooks.com

Copyright © 2008 James White

All rights reserved. No part of this book may be reproduced in any form or by any means without prior written consent of the publishers, excepting brief quotes used in reviews.

Library of Congress Cataloging-in-Publication Data

White, James (James Timothy)
  My first million : essential money tips from one of the world's youngest self-made millionaires / James White.
     p. cm.
  ISBN 978-0-8253-0586-3 (alk. paper)
  1. Finance, Personal. 2. Investments. I. Title.

  HG179.W5228 2008
  332.024'01--dc22

                                    2007047257

PRINTED IN THE UNITED STATES OF AMERICA.

To my mother and father, my brother Jeffrey, and all my friends.
Your support and encouragement have made
everything I do possible.
Thank you.

CONTENTS

My Fir$t Million

Essential Money Tips from One of the World's Youngest Self-Made Millionaires

INTRODUCTION

Congratulations on beginning your journey to better finances. By reading this book, you've already taken your first steps towards educating yourself on becoming a financially fit person.

If you are serious about increasing your earning potential, understanding how your finances work (and don't) is fundamental to creating capital. It's essential to know what's in your best interests no matter what, and invest accordingly.

Becoming wealthy always comes down to individual choices. Rarely do millionaires make one smart business decision and automatically turn into big tycoons. It's a day-to-day mentality of how you want to live your life. It's also a matter of smart, consistent investing, wise planning and dedication.

Where one person with a little extra cash may buy an expensive television, a wannabe millionaire would invest it to turn that little extra cash into a lot more. By paying attention and working hard, turning from a "thousandaire" to a millionaire may be easier than you thought.

Born and raised in Calgary, Alberta, I was raised to believe in the power of people above all else. My family did not start out rich by any means. We were a lower middle class family struggling, like many other families, to make ends meet. At four years old, I remember my mother dividing one can of tomato soup to feed four people. Seeing that struggle inspired me to work as hard as I could to support myself and my family. I cannot express the contentment I feel when I am able to take care of my own family, as a thank you for everything they've done for me.

I am not your average 23-year-old. I have spent almost my entire life learning, growing, and proving people wrong in business. Everybody has challenges when it comes to being successful and I had to overcome the stereotype associated with my youth. But now I am able to use it as a marketing tool. How many people my age have accomplished what I have? Certainly not many and that's why people trust me. I must know what I'm doing.

But the truth is, I have been building successful businesses for over a decade. It all began when I peered outside my window and noticed a person shoveling snow. Immediately the idea for a lawn care business hit me, just like that! You know, I thought, in Calgary, there will *always* be snow that needs shoveling and grass that needs to be cut.

Taking this basic "supply and demand approach" and arming myself with a $20 shovel, I started my first landscaping business at the age of

12 and began networking around my neighborhood, giving people the opportunity to meet me. I was learning firsthand the world of business development.

The trick when you are building on an idea is the growth-off-growth approach. I spent the first few years of my landscaping business putting everything I made back into the company, making it more professional. By the time I was fifteen I had invested enough money to afford large industrial equipment like heavy-duty trucks and bobcats, which meant I could offer more advanced landscaping services. The higher the level of service, the higher premium you can charge.

This business was fantastic for networking. I dealt with people all the time, making a name for myself. Through one of my clients, I was introduced to the property management business—buying and selling condominiums. Soon after, my second company came into being—J & W Property and Asset Management.

As time went on, more opportunities became apparent and I continued to build what is now a multi-million dollar enterprise (*www.jwcorporate.com*). It encompasses five companies: J&W Mechanical Fleet Services, J&W Lawn Care and Snow Removal, J&W Tire Trax Inc., Courier and Delivery Service, and J&W Property and Asset Management.

Currently I am focusing on my newest business, Canam Credit Company Inc., a multi-million dollar international enterprise. There is always a demand for alternative money solutions, especially in a big city like Calgary, and this company responds to these needs by providing business factoring and private lending.

Whether you live in a small town or big city, or hold small or large account balances, there is always space to grow and that's what I love about the financial world. Living in Calgary during an economic boom not seen since the oil growth in the 1970's has been an exciting and prosperous time and has taught me a lot about the business world.

The trick to making money anywhere is taking advantage of every opportunity and never giving up. If you're smart and more importantly, AWARE, then moneymaking possibilities start opening up everywhere. The key lies in networking. The more networking you can do, the more your name gets out there and the more people think of you when opportunity comes along.

For this reason, never forget a name! Write it down, include it in your rolodex or add it to your Christmas card list. Do whatever you have to in keeping that contact because you never know where it could lead!

INTRODUCTION

Never assume anything about a person you meet for the first time. By judging someone you could automatically be shutting a door to a chance to make lots of money. Whether the person is a customer in your business or a stranger at a party there could be an opportunity. You just need to create it by showing up.

Some people think that to be financially successful you have to give up the things you love: entertainment, time, relationships, morals, etc. It's just not true. Certainly a person's focus may change, but building success is about finding new passions and discovering new possibilities. What's important is being creative and different when it comes to business and money, and that involves changing, even creating markets where you see a demand or opportunity.

Ever heard the expression "money makes the world go round"? Well it's not 100% untrue. Think about how many times you use, think about and discuss money every day. Now think about all the areas in the financial world that you don't understand or wish to understand better.

Instead of trying to grasp overwhelming financial concepts, how about taking practical advice that you can incorporate into your everyday life? It doesn't have to be as complicated as you might think. No matter what age, location or tax bracket you happen to be in, your money has the potential to grow in ways you may not even realize.

Now I don't want to make it seem like becoming rich is easy. It isn't. It takes hard work and a smart business sense. But by becoming knowledgeable on the markets and by networking, you can eliminate many of the unknown variables and start making smarter choices when it comes to your money.

The best way to do that is by gaining access to information that will help your money grow. Though you may be well aware of your financial situation, if you're willing to learn more about the financial world around you, it's amazing how many opportunities start appear seemingly out of nowhere.

Money cannot make your dreams come true, but it can make it a lot easier to create opportunities for those dreams to become reality. Success is a completely relative term—the most important thing is to set goals and live up to all of your own expectations. I truly hope you gain whatever degree of financial prosperity you are searching for and can incorporate the things you learn in this book into your daily life.

And when you buy that first mansion or go on that dream vacation, remember me. Good luck on your pursuit!

— James T. White

BUDGETING
How to, What if, and What Now

In order to be financially successful, you need to fully understand every aspect of your money: where it comes from, where it goes, and most importantly, how you can reduce unnecessary costs. This does not have to be a difficult task. Usually it is simply a matter of a little homework, diligence, and commitment. Coming up with some kind of plan will help you in the short term and long term.

1. How do I make a personal financial plan?

Personal planning is a smart, relatively easy way to ensure (or at least increase the chances) of financial stability and progress. It is different from a budget because it can be much more vague. It is not an action, but an overview of your financial situation and doesn't set strict rules or limitations. It involves understanding your net worth, setting financial goals, and working out a basic plan to achieve them.

Sound easy? It can be, but it's usually not a quick process. Begin by writing down all of your financial goals. Break each one of these down into several short-term, medium-term, and long-term goals. Where do you see yourself in five years? How about twenty years?

Next, become educated on ways to sustain and develop these areas of your finances. This may take some time and require some reading but will pay off in the end. Evaluating your progress is essential and will show you whether or not it is working.

Remember that following a successful financial plan means being realistic and making smart money choices on a daily basis. It involves being committed and disciplined. Another obstacle to smart financial planning is procrastination. So start NOW! There is no time like the present to become financially healthy!

2. How important is a budget?

A business cannot function without a budget and neither should you. A budget lets you control your money instead of its controlling you. It will tell you whether or not you are living with in your means and help you focus on important goals.

Additionally, knowing exactly where your money is and where it is going will give you a better perspective on which direction you're heading in financially. A budget can get you out of debt and keep you there by revealing aspects of your spending that are either unnecessary or inflated, which in turn will help you sleep better at night.

Sticking to a budget will actually help you free up extra cash to save, invest, or treat yourself to something special. It will also help you prepare for those unforeseen expenses and/ or emergencies that may (and probably will) pop up.

3. What should my budget include?

Start by putting on paper how much you make, how much you spend, and how much you owe. This will give you a good overview of your financial situation and help predict any future complications.

Include any possible financial burdens that are not planned but could happen in the next year or so. This could include losing a job, health complications, an unexpected move, etc.

Next write down specific financial goals you have. Do you want to start saving for your child's education? What about a new car or a vacation getaway? A budget will help you get there and will help you stay motivated.

Keep receipts! Have a place in your home to place all credit card, gas, and food receipts, and add them up at the end of each month. If you're spending too much on food, try cooking at home more often.

Consider your outstanding debt and stick to a repayment plan. Mortgages, car loans, and business loans should all be included.

Lastly and most importantly, make your budget realistic. Life is hard and there is no sense in making it harder by living up to your own crazy expectations. If you work out a plan you can stick to, you are more likely to follow through with it in the long run.

4. How do I figure out my net worth?

Knowing your net worth is important for anyone who wants to be financially stable. No matter what your situation, figuring out where you stand financially will benefit you by giving you more control over where your money goes and will help you when applying for a mortgage, credit card, car loan, or other financial aid.

Your net worth is the difference between your assets (the things you own) and your liabilities (the things you owe). The goal is simply to have more assets than liabilities. To calculate this, get a piece of paper, a pen, and your thinking cap.

Write down the value of everything that you own, including cash (or cash equivalents), investments, real estate, household goods, retirement funds, etc. Total the value of these assets.

Next list all of your liabilities. These include loans, mortgages, credit card balances, and taxes. Total this list.

Finally, subtract your liabilities from your assets. If you have a positive number, you are doing great! If the number is *negative*, it's time to figure out what to do to change your financial situation.

When determining your net worth, make sure you include every miscellaneous item or investment that is worth money.

Everyone will have a different list, but if you are not sure you've included all your assets or liabilities, use a net-worth sample worksheet, available online or at your bank, as a checklist.

5. What are some easy ways to put aside money on a daily basis?

Believe it or not, there are some easy ways to save money every day that may not seem significant at first, but can eventually add up. When you get home from work, school, errands—wherever—put the spare change from your pocket into a jar stashed somewhere where you will always see it. It may take awhile to add up, but the benefits can be substantial and help you out when you need a few extra dollars.

Are you always being told to control your bad language? Contain that loose tongue by starting a swear jar. A quarter or a dollar owed for each bad word will add up and save you from embarrassing situations.

Have you come into a little extra cash that you know will burn a hole in your pocket? Instead of spending it, put it in the pocket of your off-season jacket. It will save you from spending it and give you a nice little surprise in a few months when you could need it more.

And keep those recyclables. Each item is worth money. You can help your bank account and help the environment at the same time.

---

6. Explain the envelope system for budgeting. How effective is it?

If you are dealing with a relatively small amount of money, this is a neat way to budget or learn the art of budgeting. It involves keeping a significant amount of cash in the house, so if you try it, purchase a fireproof safe or choose a very secret drawer to store it in.

Each time you get paid, split your cash and place into separate envelopes. How many envelopes depends on your specific needs and wants. For example, you might have one for eating out, one for clothing, one for household items, one for auto repairs, one for gifts, one for home improvements, and others for whatever else you want or need.

The envelope system is not for everyone, especially if you are not able to keep money in your house with being tempted to spend it impulsively. To see if this method is effective for your lifestyle, start small, using only one or two envelopes, and work up from there.

The disadvantage of this system is that you are not making interest on your money if it's sitting at home. (Keep in mind that you are not making much interest with it sitting in a traditional savings account either.) To have the best of both worlds, use a "virtual envelope" system. Have your money in the bank but use a spreadsheet listing your total budget and have sub-accounts for each category of expense. You can easily see where your money is going and track your progress as well.

7. How much money should I have in my emergency fund?

Life has a funny way of playing with people, and usually these games cost money. Ideally, an average person should have three to six months of basic living expenses saved up in case something unexpected happens.

You don't want a bad situation turning worse because you don't have the cash to compensate. The more dependents you have, the more you should save. Three months' salary is fine for someone single but won't last nearly as long if you're feeding a family of four.

Consider the level of difficulty you may (or may not) have in finding a new job in case you lose yours. For example, if you are a teacher and teachers are in high demand, you won't likely be unemployed for long.

The key to creating and building an emergency fund is putting a little bit aside on a regular basis. This can be arranged with your bank so you don't notice the deduction as much. Whatever your situation, set aside some money now. Doing it will save you time, energy, and one heck of a migraine later on.

8. I have automatic withdrawal payments from my bank account. Is it better to have all of my bills paid on the same day or spread the payment dates over the course of the month?

Automatic withdrawal payments can be a very convenient and an easy way to pay bills since you don't have to do anything. (Isn't it interesting, though, that the one thing banks make easy is getting rid of your money?)

When you pay bills is generally up to you and should depend on certain factors like when you get paid. If you have a regularly scheduled payday, have some (or all) of your online payments processed on the day your paycheck is deposited in the bank. That way, you won't have to worry about having an overdrawn account ever again. (Just remember to keep those paychecks higher than your bills!).

If you decide to spread your payments out across the month, stay aware of how much money you have in the bank during the course of the month.

9. I can't control my impulse buying! It seems like the more I buy, the more I want to buy! HELP!

This is actually a very common problem among people of all income levels.

One way to deal with impulse buying is to pay cash whenever possible. You can literally see the money you are spending and you are less likely to empty your wallet or purse.

Sometimes, however, that singing clown lamp in the store window is just too tempting to ignore! Instead of running inside and throwing money on the counter, wait two weeks. If you still want the item (and have the disposable income to purchase it), then go for it.

Another "trick" is to have no more than three items on a "waiting" list. If you want to add an item, require yourself to cross one item off. This will reduce your "got to have it now or I will explode" habits and will also save you from buying things you may regret later. (*Clown lamp*? What was I *THINKING*?)

10. My spouse is a habitual over-spender! How can I keep the bills paid and the fridge full?

You will find financial squabbles in every relationship. This is because people approach money and budgeting differently. Your spouse may simply not understand the importance of budgeting and need guidance. NOTE: This does NOT mean taking away his/her credit card and acting superior. In fact, get rid of the negative attitude altogether.

Try getting your partner to write down his or her life goals, and show him how the frivolous spending will never get them to where they want to be.

If you have a joint bank account, consider having enough income from his or her paycheck (assuming your partner has one) directly deposited into the joint account for bills and necessities. Get a buy-in from your spouse that the two of you will discuss any large purchases before making them.

If your spouse is unable to control her spending to the extent that you do, educate your partner as much as you can on budgeting and financial control. If both of you agree, consider taking over the finances; be careful, though, because this can cause conflict down the road.

Consider consulting with a financial planner. An objective professional can be a better resource for both of you.

NOTES:

CREDIT & YOU

Welcome to the Wonderful World of Credit

Credit can be a great thing or something to be feared, depending on your attitude. If you don't understand how credit works but use it anyway, you may be taking a lot of unnecessary risks without many rewards. If you tend to get caught up in the plastic world of credit and debit cards, then smarten up! For many in this world of convenience, credit can be just a little *too* convenient.

If you treat credit responsibly, though, and know how to use it, then you have nothing to worry about. It can benefit you throughout your life and open doors that you may not even realize. The problem most people have is they don't understand the ins and outs of the credit industry and don't know their options.

Well, here's your chance. Grab a pen!

1. Which is better: several credit cards with low balances or one credit card with a higher balance?

Your credit score could be affected if you hold several credit cards with low balances. This ultimately affects the percentage rates you are charged when you apply for loans. When banks see you with several credit cards, it sends a message that you may be desperate for credit, making you a higher risk for non-payment.

It is best to keep one credit card with a higher balance. (You can always negotiate with the credit companies to lower your monthly interest payment.)

2. What should I do with my credit card receipts?

The Internal Revenue Service has the right to review up to seven years of financial data if they conduct a personal audit. For this reason, it is a good idea to keep a file that holds all of your receipts going back seven years. Keeping these credit card transactions and other receipts may save you time, stress, and cost later on. Having all of your receipts in one place will help if there are mistakes on your statements, during tax time, or when reviewing your budget.

3. When trying to get approved, should I apply for as many credit cards as possible?

Although this practice may be tempting, avoid it, as it actually *decreases* your chances of getting approved.

For one thing, creditors look at the total unused credit line on all of your cards. If you have the ability to charge $40,000 on your credit cards but in fact only owe around $1,000, a potential creditor may regard the $40,000 spending power as if you already owed that money.

Also, when you apply for credit the issuer requests a copy of your credit report, which shows up as an inquiry on your report. Some creditors assume that many of the inquiries on your report resulted in credit granted, and may refuse to extend additional credit to you based on this assumption.

4. What is the best way to lower my credit card interest rates?

If your credit card payments are too high, debt consolidation may be for you. It won't impair your credit profile—in fact, consolidating your debt may improve your credit rating. And, if secured with real estate, the interest may be tax deductible.

Keep in mind that not all debt consolidation runs the same track. The process depends on whether you own or rent your home, your monthly income-to-debt ratio, and your current credit rating.

A less time-consuming option is to contact your credit company and tell them you're credit shopping and won't continue to pay high rates. They'll want to keep your business and will often lower the rate. If the first representative you reach declines your request, ask to speak to the credit manager. Keep climbing the chain of command. I guarantee you will save money.

While you're at it, ask them to waive any annual fees. It never hurts to ask—chances are they will if you put a little effort into it.

5. What role do credit bureaus play in an individual receiving credit?

Credit bureaus are the "gatekeepers" to the wonderful land of credit. These bureaus gather information on how you use credit and reveal to potential lenders your credit history, which supplies information from which they determine whether or not you are a credit risk. Are you able and willing to repay the credit?

There are three major bureaus in the United States: Equifax, Experian, and TransUnion.

6. How does a creditor decide if you're creditworthy?

By knowing how a creditor will evaluate you, not only is mystery removed from the process, but more importantly, you can take major steps toward improving your credit profile and increasing your chances of getting credit approved.

When you apply for credit by filling out an application, the form typically gives the creditor permission to retrieve your credit report from a credit bureau. Once this is done, the creditor assesses your credit worthiness based on both objective and subjective criteria.

Many lending institutions will employ a short-term debt-to-income ratio with which they calculate your present short-term debt payments and divide the total by your total annual income. Generally, creditors will not lend to you if your short-term debt is more than 20 percent of your annual income.

Similarly, a potential creditor will add up all your monthly bills (not including rent/mortgage and utilities) and divide by your gross income. Here, creditors are looking for a ratio of under 35 percent.

For this reason, it's a good idea to review your credit report, find any credit card accounts you no longer want, and cancel them.

Most lending institutions employ their own version of a credit-worthiness scoring system with which they assess your credit information. The number of years at your job predicts your stability and consistency, and the *kind* of work you do holds importance as well. Manual work, for instance, is seen as less favorable than clerical work. Next preferred is the self-employed, and those in managerial positions. The most favored is the almighty professional.

Creditors also look at the amount of credit you currently have. How much debt would you be in if you maxed out your present cards? Do you have a telephone in your own name? How long have you lived at your present address. Do you own your home?

The number and nature of the blotches on your credit history also send up red flags, the worst, of course, being bankruptcy.

7. What is a credit score? Why is it important?

A credit score is a single number based on your credit history that potential lenders use to determine whether or not they will extend credit to you. The number can range from three hundred to nine hundred (the higher, the better) and is calculated based on a number of factors.

It considers your payment history (including late payments, collections, bankruptcies, etc.) and your outstanding debt. The more credit you've racked up on your cards, the lower the score will be. The length of time you've had established credit is also evaluated since the more information a lender can assess, the better he can predict your repayment behavior. The types of credit you currently have figure into your credit score as well. This includes the number of loans you have and the types of accounts you hold.

A high number of inquiries on your report may lower your credit score since it reveals, in some cases, how many times you've applied for credit.

The advantage of a credit score is that it makes the process of assessing creditworthiness quick, easy, and objective for lenders. The number reveals to the lender immediately how much of a risk you are based on their company's system of assessment.

Before applying for credit, find out what your credit score is by visiting websites that provide the service or by requesting the information from a potential lender when you are applying for a loan.

8. What happens to your credit score when you get married?

Initially, nothing happens.

Once you are married, though, you may decide to apply together for a mortgage, car loan, and so on. At this point, your partner's credit (and yours) will affect whether or not you're approved and the interest rate. From that point on, whatever happens with your line of credit affects *both* of your credit scores. (Remember that whole "for richer or for poorer" thing?)

The good news is that if one of you has good credit and the other not so good, you can apply for credit separately.

9. What are the kinds of negative marks that can appear on my credit and how bad are they?

The following is a list of most of the negative items that could appear on your credit report. They are listed in order of what many creditors would consider as "best to worst."

- **Credit inquiries** – *shows how many times your report has been requested*

- **Credit rejections** – *shows how many times you've been rejected for credit*

- **Late payments** – *shows how many times you've been late with payments*

- **Past due and unpaid payments** – *shows your potential to miss future payments*

- **Court judgments** – *shows legal proceedings that may affect your credit*

- **Collections** – *shows any assets collected from you due to lack of payment*

- **Loan defaults** – *shows failure to repay a loan or violated conditions of the loan agreement*

- **Repossession** – *shows retrieval of any items purchased in order to pay back the loan*

- **Foreclosure** – *shows seizing of property that has been foreclosed upon due to financial instability or inability to pay*

- **Bankruptcy** – *shows inability to repay loans; includes chapter of bankruptcy*

10. How long does information stay on my credit report?

Timeframes depend on the type of information. In some circumstances, for example, when you are applying for life insurance with a benefit greater than $50,000, credit bureaus may supply information outside of the allocated timeframes.

Delinquent payments: Even if you later pay off an account in full, payments to creditors made over thirty days past due will remain on your credit report for three to seven years.

Collection accounts: After as few as three months of payment delinquency, a creditor may turn your account over for collections. Your credit report will reflect the collection activity for seven years from the time the first payment you missed was due. If you pay off the account after collection activity has commenced, your credit report will still be marked for seven years but may indicate "paid collection."

Inquiries: Inquiries are notations in your credit report marking a request to view it. For example, when you fill out an application for a credit card, the credit card company asks the credit bureau for a copy of your credit report, creating an inquiry notation. Most inquiries remain for two years. Note that too many inquires on your credit report can reduce your credit rating.

Charge-offs: These occur when a creditor decides to write off your debt as a loss rather than attempt to collect it from you. Such charge-offs remain on your credit for seven years from the time of the first missed payment.

Bankruptcy: Chapter 7, 11, and 12 bankruptcies remain on credit reports for ten years from the date of filing. Chapter 13 bankruptcies stay on your credit for seven years after they are discharged, which is usually three to five years after filing.

11. Does this mean I have to wait seven to ten years before I can get a loan if I have bad credit?

Although negative information stays on your credit report for up to ten years, it is possible to be approved for credit in the meantime. Creditors are much more interested in your present circumstances than what happened to you five or ten years ago.

Rebuilding your credit can be done relatively quickly through a systematic plan and a little perseverance. Keep in mind that positive credit information stays on your credit report indefinitely!

12. What if I'm turned down for credit?

By law, creditors must provide two things along with your rejection letter. They must advise you of the specific reasons for why you were rejected and give the name and address of the credit bureau they used to make the decision.

If the reason stated for rejection is inaccurate, immediately get a copy of your credit report from the bureau used and analyze it for errors. If you find a mistake, contact the bureau and supply the necessary information to fix it. Afterward, you can reapply to the same creditor, attaching an explanation and an updated copy of your credit report.

If you were rejected based on accurate data, you may still appeal the rejection by sending a letter to the creditor explaining why you are a better credit risk than your credit report may indicate.

You will probably have to jump through a few hoops and meet certain conditions in rebuilding your credit before they will approve your application. But hey, what's a little hoop jumping for credit approval?

13. Should I use a credit counseling company to help me settle my debts?

Achieving debt relief is a case-by-case circumstance.

The key is in understanding exactly where you stand regarding how much you spend, how much you make, and how much you owe. The more information you have, the easier time you'll have getting out of debt.

You can do it by yourself, but some credit counseling companies are able to get a larger debt settlement. They do this by collectively making an offer to a bank to settle much more than just your debt alone.

Working with a credit counseling company is generally less of a headache, but if it doesn't work for you, you can still try debt consolidation, debt negotiation, or as a last resort, filing bankruptcy.

14. What are the advantages of joining a credit union?

Credit unions offer loans, financial counseling, savings, and other related services. Because credit unions are member-owned, as a member, you have the power to direct policy.

Credit unions are generally a good idea. Not only are you able to pool your savings with other members, but because credit unions are not-for-profit organizations, they operate at a lower cost, assuring good rates on your saving investments and low interest rates on loans.

As well, you are entitled to run for the board of directors and attend meetings, which could help networking and teach you more about the financial world.

15. Are debit cards are good method of payment?

Debit card transactions are a popular method of payment because they involve spending money that you currently have.

Yet though it may sound crazy, if you are financially unhealthy, it may be a good idea to cut up your debit card altogether! Problems can arise from using debit cards, especially if you aren't diligent about keeping track of purchases.

Without direct access to your funds at all times, you might be surprised at how much money you save! (This applies to credit cards, too. There's no sense in spending money you neither have nor will have).

16. Are there charges for using my debit card?

Every person with a debit card has an account with specific information and limitations; some may be limited to, say, sixty transactions a month without charge. If this works for you, it's great, but if not, beware of making purchases at a small cost for each transaction above the allotted number.

If you use your debit card at an ATM that your bank is not affiliated with, there may be an even smaller limit to transactions without charge. It pays to keep track of your card transactions! Moreover, some small businesses charge a couple of dollars for very small purchases, e.g. $2 or less, made with your debit card. (If they do charge a fee, they must post a sign saying so.)

To learn more about your personal limits and exceptions, contact your bank.

17. What happens if my debit card is stolen? Am I liable for any false charges?

As soon as you discover your debit card is missing, report it to your bank and file a police report. The sooner you do this, the better.

Most banks will rebate anything over $50 in charges, and some will cover the entire cost, provided you report the card missing immediately.

DEBT/LOANS
How to Stop Digging When Living in the Hole

Most people live in debt. This doesn't have to be a huge problem in your life, as long as it is kept under control and steps are constantly being taken to lessen the gap between you and financial independence.

Debt and lending can be a scary path for most people, but it is the dedication to long- and short-term goals that makes the difference when entering into and exiting from the pitfalls of debt.

Remember to be smart when thinking about your debt situation. Consider how it affects your life, what steps you will take to alleviate the stresses that debt and loans usually bring with them, and you may discover that the situation isn't as grim and scary as you made it out to be. A little perseverance and knowledge could end up saving you tons of dough.

1. Is it better to save money or pay off debt?

Without a doubt, paying off debt is more beneficial to you because the interest you pay on debt is much greater than the interest you earn while saving money. Psychologically speaking, being debt-free will help you sleep better.

2. Should I consolidate my debt with a second mortgage?

Consolidating your debt by getting a second mortgage may result in lower overall payments, but be aware of the costs. You are required to put your home up for collateral, so if you don't keep up the payments, you may not keep your home. At the same time, home equity loans may provide you with tax advantages that you wouldn't find in other types of loans.

3. How long does it take from the time a credit card debt is past due until they turn it over to collections?

It can vary, but the general rule is anywhere between three months and seven months. Keep in mind there is statute of limitations for how long the creditor or collection agency can hassle you for the money, depending on where you live. Remember, if you let a large balance go unpaid for a long period of time, your credit score will end up being very low and will hurt your chances of future loan approvals.

4. What are the pros and cons of bankruptcy?

Bankruptcy occurs when a person in debt can no longer submit the necessary payments and creditors are unwilling to provide more credit or restructure the debt. Of course, bankruptcy should always be considered the last resort. It is a hard road to travel in achieving a financial solution, but it will get you there legally and gives you a chance at future stability.

You will have to go to court, and you may lose any assets you have, but the positives of bankruptcy are fairly clear. It enables you to legally take care of your debt, protects you from hounding creditors, and essentially gives you a fresh financial start.

But it does not come without a cost.

5. What is the difference between a fixed rate and an adjustable rate? Which one is better?

The interest percentage on an adjustable rate loan changes over time depending on how the loan is set up, whereas a fixed rate is constant over the life of the loan. What is best depends on the economic climate; lately, a fixed rate has been better because it isn't affected by fluctuations in interest rates over the course of the loan.

If you have a four-percent loan at a fixed rate for twenty years, it means you will pay 4 percent interest on the loan for 20 years. An adjustable rate varies either up or down based on the interest rate set by the Federal Reserve Board.

If the interest rate increases to 10 percent, this is what you will be paying for that period of the loan. (Keep in mind that interest rates are occasionally lowered as well.)

Exactly which of the two is better really depends on whether you are dealing with a rising-rate system (wherein fixed rates would win out by staying low) or a low-rate system, whereby an adjustable rate would be preferable. It is difficult to determine which of these two environments will prevail in the next few years because past performance is seldom an indicator.

6. I need money fast. Is borrowing from friends and family a good idea?

This depends on your family and friends. Generally, your support system is a good place to go when you need any kind of help, and if your friends and family know you well enough, they will decide for themselves whether you are worth the risk of lending money. Many times these people will forgo interest payments, which can save you money. However, lending from family and friends can end up getting ugly and ruining relationships. Too many of these cases end up in small-claims court, so tread lightly and act responsibly.

Here are a few pointers that you should keep in mind to protect yourself from grief.

Step 1: DON'T GET EMOTIONAL! Leave financial agreements out of any other squabble or argument you may have.

Step 2: Get everything in writing. People, no matter how good their intentions are, are fallible. Getting all the details and numbers down on paper protects everybody from forgetfulness or disagreements. This helps the process go smoothly, especially if the relationship ends during the repayment process.

Step 3: Decide on an official plan of repayment, including a completion date.

Step 4: Pay the person back! You do not want to be "that friend" whom nobody loans money to; that person usually ends up lonely and poor.

7. My friend/family member asked me for a loan, but he/she doesn't have the greatest history with money. What can I do to ensure I get my money back?

When lending money to a person who is close to you, treat the process just as if you were lending to a stranger. This helps things from getting emotional and protects you from being taken advantage of.

Since you do not have the luxury of directly withdrawing money from the person's bank account, you have to depend on him or her to pay you. If you are not sure whether the person can do that, reconsider making the loan.

Or you can help protect your position by setting up a contract with the person, stating all the details of the lending agreement, including a repayment schedule and any interest rates, and having each party agree to the terms, and sign the document.

The process of repayment can be flexible, making a payment every week, bi-monthly, monthly, etc. Whatever it is, make sure it is realistic in order to avoid problems! You are the banker in this situation, so be strong and don't let your friend or family member weasel out of anything!

If both parties are responsible and respectful of each other, the process will go off without a hitch and you will feel great for helping out a friend in need.

8. What should I know before I co-sign a loan?

As a co-signer for a loan, you are basically lending some-body your good credit to obtain a loan. If the person you co-sign for begins to miss payments, the creditors will come after you—you are held accountable for the money.

You should always be very cautious when thinking about co-signing anything. Make sure you back yourself up finan-cially.

Let's say you co-sign a loan for property. If you aren't sure the person is financially stable enough, you might consider buying the property yourself and renting it to them until they can afford to buy. Or split the payments for the property. That way if the signer does not come through with the payments, you at least have some ownership rights.

Whatever the situation, the most important thing to re-member is whether or not the person you are co-signing for is credible. Assess the risk honestly. Everybody makes mistakes in their past and many have streaks of bad luck, but beyond that you don't want to mess with your credit without having done anything to affect it adversely yourself.

9. I just received a hefty inheritance. What should I do with the money?

Depending on the amount of the inheritance, there are some smart ways to invest your money and make long-term plans. Assuming it is a large inheritance, setting up an emergency fund (upwards of $10,000) is a great start. You could increase your 401(k) contribution and put some aside for your child's education.

Your mortgage: to pay or not to pay? The answer depends on the interest rate you're paying. If it's low, you can probably find a better investment that could give you a higher return. Otherwise, pay it off instead of having your money sit in a savings account with a very low interest rate.

CUTTING COSTS
Easy Saving Tips

SPEND LESS MONEY THAN YOU MAKE. It's a simple enough statement to say, but not so simple to live by. Many people get caught up in the spending game and forget about the consequences of living beyond their means.

A good way to live within your budget and still have many of the things you love is by trimming costs. Sometimes spending more, especially when you can't afford it, is just plain dumb. The one thing every person should know about his or her financial life is that saving money does not have to be hard. *Inconvenient? Time-consuming? Boring?* Sure. *Difficult?* No way.

In fact, there are ways to save money every day that take no effort at all—short-term adjustments for long-term objectives. Begin by reviewing where your money's going. If the things you're spending money on are really worth it. If they aren't, trim the fat and chances are your life won't be much different—just richer.

Many people struggle with saving money in the short term because they don't see the savings right away. A few cents off a gallon of milk today may not be much, but think of it over a year's time!

43

1. How can I cut costs on food?

Food is a necessary expense; don't feel guilty or worried about spending money on the things that will keep you alive! The trick is being smart about where you're spending it and how you can avoid spending more money than you have to.

Consider the grocery store. Clipping coupons is always a penny-saving venture and is usually worth the effort in the long run. Some stores have double- or triple-coupon days, which can make a difference. Make a shopping list that you can stick to prior to visiting the grocery store (no more impulse buying), and never go food shopping when you're hungry! Your financial priorities tend to waiver when temptation is all around you.

Do not eat out or order in food often. The convenience will cost you big money in the long run. Fruits, vegetables, and basic food ingredients are usually inexpensive, so buy in bulk and make your own meals at home; make extra so there are leftovers for lunch and some you can freeze. By using vegetables that you've grown and doing the cooking yourself, you save money, and who knows—maybe you'll discover the chef within!

To cut down on the cost of drinks, avoid expensive name brands. Also cut down on alcohol. You will save a bundle of money and feel great, too. Drink water when you can. (You're paying for it anyway.) Try keeping a jug of water in your fridge so there is always a cheap alternative when you're thirsty.

Lastly, compare store prices. Look through flyers (some stores even post their flyers on their websites) or try different stores and compare in person. Though this may seem time-intensive, the effort you put in will definitely save you money!

2. How can I save money when eating out?

When eating in a restaurant, there are tips you can use to keep from spending a fortune while still enjoying a night out. Check local newspapers for coupons or deals for restaurants you've been dying to try. If the restaurant is expensive, try visiting for lunch or dessert. The prices are usually lower then, and you still get the experience of a fancy restaurant.

Ask if there are half-portions available on menu items, and don't be afraid to take food home for lunch the next day.

Be aware of what you're drinking. Alcohol can be very expensive, so if you don't care what you're drinking, go with water with lemon or lime. Try not to eat out often, as this will certainly create a dent in your budget!

3. How can I avoid spending lots of money on clothing?

Nobody says you have to shop at premium, top-dollar stores for your clothing. If you are looking to save a buck or two, there are many second-hand stores that offer cheap and eclectic fashions for all shapes and sizes. The assortments change often too, so if you can't find anything you like, try again in a week.

If you are strapped for cash, there are charitable services that can help you, like the Salvation Army, Goodwill, or your local church.

If you are looking to simply resist your shopaholic tendencies, try skipping the brand new "must-have" accessories. What is popular today is old news tomorrow, so save on your credit card debt.

If you can sew or know somebody who can, then go nuts! Get creative and make repairing or altering your clothes a fun new hobby!

4. What about shelter? How can I cut costs?

With shelter, it's a little more difficult to cut costs. The unexpected will occur. If the furnace breaks or the pipes burst, you can't ignore it or cover it up with duct tape. But there *are* a few ways to reduce costs.

Begin by setting up a house emergency fund for any problems that come up that you cannot fix yourself. When something does need repairing, do your research and compare contractors. They are in direct competition with each other and their rates are relatively fluid.

Get the best price. This doesn't necessarily mean the *lowest* price, however. You want the work done properly and as the old adage says, you get what you pay for.

If you are looking to remodel, take your time and do each room on its own. Spread out the cost and save yourself a headache.

5. How can I save money on air conditioning?

A little awareness and some common sense go a long way when the energy bill arrives.

There are several ways to reduce the costs of cooling your home. Begin by investing in the right air conditioner, and make sure that it is serviced properly to ensure efficient use. Look for one that has a SEER number (seasonal energy efficiency ratio) of 13 or better.

If you're shopping for a window air-conditioning unit, know that size doesn't equal cost efficiency! Base the size of the machine on the size of the room, and remember not to block it with furniture.

Program your thermostat so that your air-conditioner doesn't run at full capacity while you're away. Install awnings on the sunny side of your house, or close the curtains.

Plant trees and shrubs around your house to reduce the heat from the sun while cutting costs up to 30 percent.

Close the cooling ducts and doors to rooms you aren't using and be aware of items in your home that generate heat—office equipment, lighting, cooking equipment, dishwashers, and clothes washers.

6. What are some ways to save money on heating costs?

Heating your home is usually necessary, and if you live in a cold climate, you know how expensive it can be. Luckily there are some simple ways to cut costs without spending a dime.

You don't have to heat every room in your house, so shut the doors and vents to rooms you barely use. In the rooms you do spend time in, turn down the heat and use space heaters instead.

Washing clothes in cold water helps, and by cutting your shower time a little, you can actually save up to 33 percent on your hot water costs! Keep your curtains open so the sun can shine in and heat your home naturally. And remember, if you are ever a little chilly, putting on a warm sweater is much cheaper than turning up the thermostat. (You can even put it in the clothes dryer for a few minutes to really get cozy!)

By following these tips, you'll be sure to get those warm, fuzzy feelings when your heating bill arrive.

7. How can I save on energy costs?

There are lots of easy ways to reduce energy in your home that will save you money and have you feeling clever for doing so.

Turn off your clothes dryer about ten minutes before the end of the cycle. You'll save money and your clothes will continue to dry in the warm machine.

If something minor breaks around the house, try fixing it yourself. Just because you've never done it before doesn't mean you can't! With some research and a little confidence, you may end up saving lots of money you might have spent on professionals. (Otherwise, keep close the number of a friend who does handiwork. Friends are always cheaper than hired help.)

Check your appliances. Your computer screen, for example, uses up more than half the energy of the computer itself, and a 17-inch computer screen uses 35 percent more energy than a 14- inch screen, so use the smallest screen that fits your need, and turn it off when it's not in use. Another thing to keep in mind is that a chest freezer is more energy-efficient than a stand-up one because the stand-up one lets cold air escape when you open the door.

8. How can I save money on my phone bill?

In this age of portable everything, it is easier than ever to keep chatting everywhere you go, but a plan that works for your neighbor may not work for you.

Keep in mind that landlines (phone lines connected to your house) may operate a little differently than cell phones because they usually involve different service providers.

Sit down with your phone statements from the last two to three months and figure out your talking patterns. How much is long-distance? What time of day do you talk the most? Once you have a good idea of your phone habits, contact your telephone company and have them help you pick a plan that works best. Some plans provide cheaper rates in the evenings and weekends, others for long-distance calls.

Another idea is to buy a phone card to keep on hand when you need it. Because of the competition in service providers, there are always new plans out there, so shop around and you can end up saving lots of money.

If you are a fan of sending text messages on your cell phone but hate the high prices, you can sometimes send free texts via the Internet. Just go to the phone provider's website and type it out. Your friend will receive the message on his or her phone at no cost to you!

Think of your service provider as working for you, and you'll have a much easier time when that bill comes your way.

9. Gas is getting more expensive by the day! Is there any way to predict when prices will go up?

Wouldn't it be great if you had a warning at the pump telling you when to fill up before gas prices skyrocket? Well, in case your crystal ball is broken, here are some tips to help you save some cash.

Though it is extremely difficult to predict and fluctuates day to day, the price of gas is a commodity just like everything else and is subject to similar factors. Rising prices, inflation, and tax laws (past and present) can all be studied to generally predict how the gas trend will continue.

Not a math whiz? You don't need graphs and laser pointers to figure out that it's all about supply and demand. Demand is steadily rising due to the increase in population and number of cars per household.

A smart way to save money on gas is to check the Internet. Many cities have sites that track local gas prices so you can compare and track where the cheapest price is that day. Stock up! If you find a great price for gas, fill up a proper container before the price jumps back up. (Keep in mind it could always go lower, too.) The thing to remember is that the higher the demand and competition, the higher the price of gas. This is why stations in large cities often charge more than smaller towns.

10. What are some more ways I can cut down on fuel costs?

There are many ways to save money on gas and avoid lining up at the gas station more often than you have to. In fact, just by making sure your vehicle is properly maintained, you can trim up to 10 percent off your fuel costs. Low tires, dirty oil, clogged air filters, and poorly tuned engines all increase your gas consumption. By using a block heater on cold winter days, you can save as much as 10 to 20 percent on fuel costs!

When you are on the road, have a plan to go everywhere you need to in one trip, while remembering not to idle. Never underestimate the benefits of carpooling! You could potentially save $400-$700 a year.

Lastly, you can always purchase vehicles that aren't gas-powered, or run on a low amount of gas. A hybrid car specializes in saving fuel consumption, and for short trips to the grocery store, a scooter or bicycle may be a good investment for you. Get exercise while saving on fuel!

11. Are there ways to buy cheap air travel tickets?

If you're looking to buy airfare but are turned off by the prices, don't worry just yet. There are ways to lower the cost of your airfare and make the best out of a usually expensive situation.

First, by booking your flight in advance and being flexible with your dates you can take advantage of seat sales. If you travel on slow days—Tuesdays and Wednesdays usually—or stay over on a Saturday, this, too, will help lower costs.

If you are looking to go on vacation, it will save you a bundle if you travel in the off-season. (It helps you avoid crowds, too.) If you can, travel on late flights in coach (a little less leg room, a lot less money). Avoiding direct travel will save you cash, too.

When booking your flight, tell the reservation clerk you are willing to be bumped to the next available flight. For getting on the following flight, you will receive a cash discount voucher for a future flight. Offer to go standby on sold-out flights. Chances are you will get a seat anyway and you'll pay a lot less for it.

These suggestions may sound a little inconvenient, but in the long run these tips could end up saving you hundreds of dollars in just one trip. Imagine how much you would save on every trip you take! You could fly yourself somewhere nice with the money you save!

12. What are some smart ways to save money on shopping retail?

The trick to saving money while still getting the things you want lies in a little advanced planning. High demand equals high prices, so consider the time of year in relation to all of your purchases.

Spring and summer merchandise usually goes on sale in June or July and fall and winter items usually are put on the clearance shelves around January, so be smart and do your shopping then. Besides, in the winter you probably already know whether you need a lawnmower, so don't procrastinate or it'll cost you!

Try shopping online to cut down on costs. There are plenty of sites that offer overstocked merchandise or retail and grocery stores that offer their services online. Not only do you save on time and gasoline, but you can even enter in promotion or coupon codes and save money while still in your living room!

13. Is it better to lease or own a car?

This depends on how long you intend to use the car. When you lease, you are not paying for the car itself. You're paying for its projected depreciation while in your use.

Typically, lease lengths range from 24 to 48 months. Many people who lease eventually pay more because they focus only on the monthly payments and not on the car's worth.

Leasing usually comes with mileage restrictions, not to mention security deposits. And once you turn in your leased vehicle, there are several fees including "wear and tear" and a payment for driving more than what was allotted in the mileage agreement.

Many times leasing isn't the cheapest way to go. If you can't afford to buy the car you're after, you can purchase it with a long-term loan, which is generally less costly than leasing. You can also consider buying an older used car.

As with any large purchase, understanding the deal before you sign anything is essential to driving away in confidence. Study the agreement and if you have any questions, ask! Jargon and technical aspects of the agreement may be confusing, so do not let the salesperson talk around or above you. This is *your* deal, *your* vehicle, and *your* money!

14. Is hiring an accountant to do my taxes worth the money, or am I better off grinding through it myself?

It depends on how experienced you are in regard to the IRS tax system and how complicated your taxes get. Generally speaking, I would hire a professional to do your taxes, as it's their profession and you want your taxes done right, especially if you have a complicated tax return.

If you have a basic return, you can buy a program and do it yourself for much less, but you may have to wait for your refund check to come in the mail and this could take a long time. If you need the money right away, go use a tax professional who can get you a check at the same time as filing your tax return.

15. I am expecting a baby. How will this affect my finances?

As the saying goes, parents are those who carry around pictures of their kids in their wallets, right where their money *used* to be. It's true that a bundle of joy can also bring with it a bundle of expenses, so the more you can do to prepare and be aware of these expenses, the better off you are.

A new baby can "cost" as much as $32,000 for the first two years alone, so it's a good idea to know what you're getting into before you become a parent. These expenses include everything from cribs to day care, to food, to diapers. Obviously having a new small relative in the house is not cheap! Try to save up for this life change, or consider a new budget for living once the new little one arrives. And don't expect them to get any cheaper. Depending on your lifestyle, a child can cost up to $10,000 a year or more until the age of 17!

16. A baby is expensive! What can I do to reduce these costs while still providing a good upbringing?

Being a parent is enough hard work without having to worry about financial strains as well. This is where forward-looking arrangements come into play.

In the United States, maternity leave benefits last up to six months; in Canada up to one year. Consult your HR professional regarding any company-provided benefit plans that have to do with infant care and pediatric coverage. Enrolling in one can significantly reduce out-of-pocket expenses and lessen the worry when and if your child needs medical attention.

If you are expecting a child, you have almost nine months to make a realistic and reasonable financial plan. A smart way to reduce costs when expecting or raising a small child is obvious. Hand-me-downs and thrift-store items are a great way to cut costs and second-hand stores offer discounts on anything from cribs to clothing to toys. Your baby will not know or care if his or her crib has had a previous owner; neither should you.

You can make your own baby food (which is also healthier) and your own baby furniture. (Nothing says "I love you" like a homemade mobile!)

If you need day care, find out if there is a less costly (but certified) childcare provider in your community. This will be cheaper and more convenient for you on a day-to-day basis.

Truth be told, any expense you incur with regard to your baby can be easily justified and will always be worth the price you pay for having a baby. (The same can be said for childbirth, but let's not go there!) What is most important to decide is what your baby needs versus what you want the baby to have. Spoiling your child when you do not have the means to do so doesn't help anything and is actually a common cause for debt problems, so don't let it happen to you.

INCREASING EARNING POTENTIAL

Why Make Some
When You Can Make More?

Are you not making enough? Do you ask yourself how you could make more money without sacrificing time and effort? Of course you have; we *all* have. We've all had that dream of the money tree growing in the backyard that would solve all of our financial woes. This tree may not exist (if you find one, let me know), but there are practical, effective ways to increase what you make without making huge life adjustments.

1. How can I increase my earning potential while already working full time?

Do you have too many bills and not enough hours in the day? There are several smart ways to fix this without losing sleep.

If you are too busy to tackle a part-time job, try starting a small home-based business that doesn't require much time. You can turn a hobby into a profit and have fun working on your own terms. This takes commitment, some time, energy, and a little know-how, so if that isn't for you, try upgrading your education.

Taking night or weekend courses is a great way to increase your earning potential because you can build your resume and learn different ways to become successful as well as open doors you never knew existed. Education is always a good investment and can be enjoyable too.

2. Is pawning my possessions a good way to make some quick cash?

Having an out-of-money experience? Though pawning your things is definitely a quick way of making some money, it is probably not the best way.

If you want to sell your possessions, chances are your friends or family would buy them from you for more money than a pawn shop would offer. If you intend to buy back your possessions, the money has to come from somewhere, and pawn shops usually charge a high interest rate.

If you decide to sell your things to a pawn shop, keep in mind there is no such thing as a good deal!

3. How important is personal image in creating business opportunity?

Recent studies show that our behavior and the way we conduct business can be attributed in part to unknown processes. That is why the first impression we make is always important.

Eye contact is integral when making business deals. It shows you are personable, trustworthy, and confident in your ability. A person is more likely to trust and invest money in somebody if they like him or her as a person.

After eye contact, hygiene plays an active role in your business appeal. If you send out the wrong signals, like body odor, cigarette smoke, or even foot smell, you may transmit a negative picture without even knowing why.

The image you project also depends on your speech, so be aware of your audience at all times. It's nice to be funny, but everyone has a different sense of humor, so be careful. You do not want to offend people you want to conduct business with you. Unfortunately, most won't tell you exactly why and you'll be destined to make the same mistakes time and time again.

4. What effect does my health have on my financial status?

This is a very complicated question. Speaking generally, physical fitness can affect your financial fitness in a number of ways.

First of all, habits like drinking and smoking can make you less of a performer at work. People with "hangovers" generally don't perform as well as they do with a good night's sleep.

The costs add up too. If, for example, you buy a $5 pack of cigarettes every day, it would cost you $1,800 a year. Likewise with alcoholic beverages. That's just under $4,000 a year!

In addition, your diet can have a great deal to do with your focus and attitude in the workplace. Candy and fast food will make you crash and burn, but taking fruits and vegetables to eat throughout the day will actually keep you focused and energized. (An apple will actually wake you up more effectively than a cup of coffee!)

Though it is certainly not necessary for a person to be physically fit to be financially fit, a healthy person exudes confidence and energy that can lead to prosperous opportunities.

5. What advice can I give my children to make sure they become financially independent?

Healthy financial habits are best taught through example.

For younger children, set up a piggy bank. If they want something, a bicycle for example, place a picture of one on the piggy bank and celebrate when they reach their goals. Have them count their savings every month or so to demonstrate their accumulation.

Match or add to the amount your child saves. Add "interest" payments to their savings, offering, for example, a dollar for every ten dollars they save. Your child will learn the basics of interest, as well as stay motivated to save money.

Once your children get older, put a savings chart on the fridge tracking how much they need to save in order to achieve their financial goals. This will act as a visual reminder. Take them to the bank and let them set up a savings account, using the opportunity to explain the process to them.

Encourage them to perform chores around the house for an allowance, such as mowing the lawn, shovelling snow, etc. By incorporating incentives for earning money, children will learn the value of what they earn and will more likely go on to work hard in the real world toward achieving these same ends.

6. What are some different kinds of unclaimed property?

Has a friend ever repaid you twenty dollars you forgot you had lent them? Wouldn't it be nice to experience that surprise on a potentially much larger scale? The truth is there may be hundreds of dollars worth of property or money that you are entitled to.

Unclaimed property most often comes about because of changes of address, changes of name (due to marriage), or sometimes the death of the owner.

Unclaimed property can include the following:

- Dormant Savings and Checking Accounts and Certificates of Deposit,

- Safe Deposit Box Contents

- Uncashed Money Orders, Cashiers Checks, and Travellers Checks

- Uncashed Payroll Checks

- Unused Gift Certificates

- Oil and Gas Royalty Payments

- Uncashed Stock and Mutual Fund Dividends -Stock Certificates

- Mineral Royalty Payments

- Unclaimed Security Deposits

- Utility Deposits

- Customer Deposits, Overpayments, Credit Balances, and Refunds

- Court Deposits

- Insurance Payments

- Probate Court Judgments

- Overlooked Property

- Paid-Up Life Insurance Policies

- Uncashed Death Benefit Checks and Life Insurance Proceeds

- Health and Accident Insurance Payments

7. How can I find out if there is unclaimed money or property owed to me?

Even if you are certain nothing is owed to you, it may be worth the short amount of time it takes to check. You can call or write the unclaimed property office in each province or state in which you or any of your deceased relatives have lived. You can sometimes also contact these offices online.

A representative will ask you for your name, social security number, address, and any previous addresses where you've lived in that area.

If there is a match, you simply have to prove that you are who you say you are, and behold! You have just claimed your money with no charge!

In addition, if the search comes up with nothing, try again in a few years. You never know what you could be missing out on. A warning: do not pay someone a finder's fee for locating your lost property! If the process is this simple, why give up a percentage of your entitlement? It may be more convenient, but the commission can be outrageous.

8. Are there government grants for the average person? How can I get one?

Grants are not provided simply to fatten your wallet or pay off debt. There are obligations that accompany each grant, but yes, they are available to almost anyone.

There are obvious obstacles, however. The number of government grants is small and competition is massive. Be prepared with a business plan and clearly defined goals.

You must apply for a grant through a grant office, supplying information about your objectives for the money. A review of your proposal will usually be conducted through a committee, with a comparison of your proposal to similar ones that also need to be reviewed.

Success in accessing a grant is contingent on a number of factors. Grants are given out to non-profit organizations, local governments, and target groups with specific requirements such as transportation.

9. How can I make money off of my vehicle?

I doubt there are many ways you can literally make money off of your vehicle, as this is an asset that depreciates in value the second you drive it off the lot. However, there are some opportunities.

For example, you can always deliver pizza or newspapers, or provide a service for elderly people or people otherwise unable to drive, providing trips to the grocery store, pharmacy, school, and other places.

10. What are some ways to make money online?

For those who know how to harness it, the power and opportunity the Internet has to offer is massive and still has room to grow. The Web offers a plethora of opportunities to make money, but the trick is to recognize the legitimate ways versus the scams.

Just as with any other moneymaking venture, you must be aware of what you are doing. First you can sell things on the Net via sites like Ebay, which offers online auctions. They're a great way to spring clean and can turn into a lucrative hobby.

Teaching online can be profitable as well, but most likely you must partner with a local school or university.

If you own a company or small business, the possibilities of making money online become even greater. If you don't have a website of your own or want to expand your demographic, there are sites that will help sell your product.

11. I have a great idea for a new invention that will make me rich! What do I do now?

Looking to revolutionize the world with your new invention?

Having an idea for a product that will make you money is great, but it won't get you rich. The truth is, if you ask, most people have at least one or two ideas of their own. The trick is to first find out if people would buy it and then get up off the couch and do something about it.

First you need a patent. A patent is a legal document that ensures the inventor (you) the exclusive right to commercially develop and distribute a product for the life of the patent, excluding others from making or distributing it.

To get a patent, you need to make sure there isn't already an invention like yours out there. Certain websites offer search archives with this information, including the governmental patent office near you.

Patenting a product can be a lengthy and confusing process, so be ready for it, and it is just the first step. Next comes research and development, engineering, commercialization, and distribution. And you need money for all of it.

Generally speaking, creating and developing an invention is not for the faint of heart, but if you are committed to doing it, then do as much research on the industry as possible and go for it.

12. What are some types of charitable donations that qualify for tax exemptions?

There are many tax credits that apply when donating to a charity, though the charity must qualify for taxation purposes, which is easy enough to find out on the Internet or through the association itself.

The donations are added to other personal credits under the Income Tax Act and are deducted directly from taxes owed. You can deduct donations of cash, real estate, vehicles, residual interest, insurance policies, mileage, and lottery funding.

Tax benefits work as incentives for donations, so if you have an old car or are just feeling generous, keep charitable associations in mind!

For more information, visit *www.irs.gov*.

13. I won the lottery! Woo hoo! But it's divided so I only get a little bit each year. Is there anything I can do to get all the money at once?

It's your lucky day. The way normal settlements work—and this applies to lotteries, lawsuit claims, any large contractual amount—is you receive your funding in stages. Say you won $25 million; it could work out that you would receive $1 million a year for twenty-five years. If that works for you, then great! Enjoy!

But if you don't want to wait for twenty-five years or you find that $20 million dog collar too hard to resist, then there is a way to speed up the entire process and claim your money now.

Private lending institutions like some credit companies provide a service of structured settlements. You sign with them and the institution will give you all the money right on the spot! However, these places usually take a little off the top for commission, so you might end up with $24 million instead. So basically it's up to you.

14. I am a full-time university student. How can I make or save money?

Being a university student can take up a lot of your time. However, if you can get a part-time job without having it interfere with your schoolwork, give it a shot. There are many job opportunities right on campus that are convenient. Otherwise, if you want to make money, you've got to get creative.

Assuming you are not worried about student loans and you simply want to make money to save or spend, concentrate on ways to save on books. Campus prices are ridiculously expensive, so share with a classmate or try finding the same books at stores off campus or even online to save costs. Also, sell your textbooks back to the school at the end of each course. Chances are you will never reference them again (unless they are applicable to other courses), and you can clear up some space in your dorm room or home.

Depending on what major you hold, you can try borrowing class books from the campus library instead of buying them. This can save you hundreds of dollars over a few years. University is a time to feel independent, so make sure you focus on a financial plan to help you do just that. Chances are if you start saving now, you will have a better chance at saving when you're older.

FINANCES & THE WORKPLACE

How to Keep Your Income Incoming

A large part of maximizing your income potential comes from your attitude. There will be times when you will be fully justified in quitting on the spot or will feel the money you make just doesn't equal the amount of suffering you put up with. These are the times when you should be most aware of factors you may not at first consider. In fact, your emotions have more to do with your workplace stability than your job skills.

How do people perceive you? How do you perceive others? How much room do you have to be creative or flexible in your work? These all contribute to your job satisfaction and will affect your long-term standing in your workplace. Employees should love what they do. But sometimes this doesn't mean they love what they're getting paid.

In times like these, you should keep in mind that there is more to income than simple salary. In fact, there are ways to increase your earning potential in the workplace without all that nasty hard work and overtime. It doesn't matter what industry you work in. You can begin making the money you want by being aware of your opportunities to assure financial stability long after you have to worry about working at all.

1. What do successful businesses look for when reviewing an applicant?

Every business seeks out different things when considering an applicant for a position. The person must be a good fit for the company, so research a company and the job before you enter an interview.

Know what they are looking for. This shows you are interested in the position and consider your work seriously. Depending on the industry, you may need to concentrate on purely professional experience, whereas attitude and personality play a major role if you are applying for a job in the service industry.

Generally, however, there are some quick dos and don'ts that always apply. DO be on time. DO be polite. DO dress nicely and cleanly. This applies to your general hygiene as well. Your first question SHOULD NOT be, "How much does it pay?" This shows your priorities are to yourself, not to the company.

As for the resume, different employers look for different things but experience is always an asset. Remember to include dates, names, and places. Commensurate educational background is a must for most businesses, and you should also include any scholarships or awards you've received. Include as well any interests or hobbies you may have. It shows the employer that you are well rounded and fun. Include as well a reference sheet, or make one available upon request. These should not be names of family or friends, but include past employers or anybody who can vouch for past working experience.

Include any information relevant to the business on your resume and include a cover letter introducing yourself to the employer and why you are interested in the job. And then, to really make yourself stand out above the other interviewees, send a letter to the interviewer thanking him for his time a day or two after the meeting.

2. In a job interview, how do you answer that inevitable question, "What are your weaknesses?"

Almost every interview you will go to will include some version of this question. Strengths are easy, but when answering a question about your "weaknesses," the trick is to be honest without trapping yourself in a corner.

Say something that is true and specific but wouldn't really apply to the job you are applying for. A great answer is "I work myself too hard," "I take my job too seriously sometimes," or my personal favorite, "I am a perfectionist!"

Never say anything like "I can't work with other people" or "I am never on time." That's like saying "Goodbye. I'm completely incompetent."

A good idea is to note that you are constantly working on your weaknesses and use them as a way to improve yourself. The interviewer will respect you for being honest, and you don't end up looking like a weak employee.

3. I'm going to ask my boss for a raise. How should I prepare?

Asking your employer for a pay increase can be a very nerve- racking and stressful chore, but every once in awhile you need to take off the gloves and get dirty.

You are essentially selling yourself and your abilities to someone who may not necessarily want to shell out extra company cash, so be diligent, confident, and above all, professional.

Always do your research prior to confrontation. Find out what other people in your field are making. (It's not exactly kosher to ask your peers, so look online for industry standards.)

Next evaluate how financially sound your employer is. The easiest thing a boss can say to turn you down is that they just don't have the cash. Knowing the financial health of a business can tell you when a good time to ask would be, and any financial research you gather could help you in arguing your case.

Next step: Decide what you're worth. Consider the amount of years you have spent with the company and any extra responsibilities you have taken on without compensation. List these duties as well as the relevant skills that make you successful at your job.

The next thing you should consider is what you are willing to do if you're turned down or are given a smaller raise than expected. Are you going to quit your job? (This information is for you. Don't give your boss an ultimatum. This is negative confrontation and does not make you look smart or professional.) If there are specific reasons as to why you were turned down, consider any changes you can make to elevate your job performance and ask to review the situation in time.

Finally, make an appointment with your boss. (You never want to bombard him or her in the hallway or cafeteria.)

Be aggressive yet positive, confident and focused. Good luck!

4. I'm too scared to ask for a raise! What are some things I can do around the office to motivate my boss into noticing me?

I'm assuming this question does not include the working-hard solution.

Truth be told, there are some tricks that can put you on the top of the boss's list, without working your fingers to the bone or even being the staff suck-up.

If you work in an office environment, always be on time and keep an active, up-to-date schedule of what you're working on. That way if you are ever interrogated about a project you worked on three weeks ago, you can spill out details easily!

Many offices re-evaluate compensation as a part of their annual performance reviews. If they don't, then mention it. They won't fire you for asking.

Get to know your boss, even if it means spending time out of the workplace. This will depend on the boss you have, but it will not only give you an advantage in knowing what your boss is looking for specifically, but it will let him or her know that you take a personal interest in his or her life.

Don't get *too* personal, however. You don't want to overstep any boundaries! And if you run your own business, then you *are* your own boss, so stop reading and give yourself a raise already!

5. What should I be aware of when setting up a retirement plan?

You should begin by assessing your life situation. Find out if your place of work has a pension or retirement plan in place and whether or not you are eligible.

Next, find out how much these plans are estimated to be worth when you will retire. This will tell you how much you need to save, if at all, in addition to these benefits.

Does your employer offer a matching contribution to your retirement plan? If so, contribute what you can because it will one day offer a 100 percent return!

Also, find out what happens to your company retirement plan if you change jobs. Sometimes these benefits can be transferred into an IRA or cashed in.

Lastly, discuss whether or not your health and life insurance policies are active once you retire, and consider whether or not your Social Security benefits could reduce your retirement benefits. Discuss this with your employer.

Finally, your retirement plan should be reviewed periodically to ensure it is working the way you need it to. The closer you get to retirement age, the more aware you should be of how your plan is performing. The sooner you work these issues out, the less you'll have to worry about when you do retire, so don't procrastinate!

6. I'm ready to retire. What now?

Finally going to retire? Congratulations! Now consider a few things to help ease you into the life of active luxury.

Start by reviewing your original retirement goals. Do they still apply? Any illnesses or investment plans can alter your initial expectations.

Look at your income. Is it more or less than what you originally set up in your plan? Also consider any outside or additional income to invest.

Evaluate your current spending habits. You may have changed the way you spend money since you set up the plan, so either alter your spending or alter your plan.

Next review your investment portfolio. As you are getting ready to retire, it is a good idea to know just how well those investments are performing.

Finally, request a statement of earnings from the Social Security Administration. This will tell you how much you can expect to earn during retirement and reveal any mistakes in your account.

7. What are some tips to consider if I lose my job?

Being prepared for financial crisis does not mean being paranoid. It's a smart idea to work out a forward-looking plan regarding what could happen if you suddenly lost your job.

If you haven't figured out your financial situation, do so, and make sure to include an emergency fund that would get you through at least three months worth of basic expenses.

Then compare it against your job stability. Is your job secure? How in demand is it? How easy would it be to find a new job?

Next inquire about your job's severance policies and other benefits that you are entitled to if you are laid off. If you do lose your job, do not burn your bridges, as much as you might like doing so! Apply for unemployment insurance as soon as possible. Also resist the temptation to charge every little thing on your credit card!

Finally, keep your job search organized and efficient. It may take time to find new financial sources, so be aggressive in your search and stay motivated.

THE BANK & YOU

Understanding Your Savings

The relationship you have with your bank can say a lot about your finances. Do you trust the bank to make financial choices? How much control do you really have over your money? What are your interest rates and how can you make them better?

Your bank must always work toward your best interests. Sometimes simply knowing which questions to ask can save you lots of money.

1. What are the advantages and disadvantages of having a bank savings account?

A savings account is a safe place to put your money. It is easily accessible when you need it and there are no fees or minimum balances.

It can also link directly to your checking account, enabling you to transfer funds between the two or have bills paid directly from the account.

The only real disadvantage of a savings account is that the interest rate is generally lower than other investment vehicles. (low risk = low return).

2. How long do I keep old bank statements?

If you are self-employed, you should keep all bank statements accounting for seven years.

Otherwise, keep them for three years. Have a safe place for them and keep them organized in case you need to reference them later on.

3. Why do governments audit people? Is it a completely random process?

Government auditing is a very detailed examination of financial records to check the accuracy of those records. The process verifies a person's transactions and financial statements, making sure there are no outstanding discrepancies.

A certain number of people or organizations are more likely to get audited, including lending institutions that contribute to or are active in federally-sponsored loan programs such as education and housing.

In every audit, the auditor must abide by the government auditing standards, which generally include responsible overview of Internet control, consistency review, recommendations for corrective action, and proper reporting procedures.

Random audits do happen, but you are more likely to be audited if you have returns that vary from year to year or all of a sudden receive a large refund, for example. Software and staff are developed to spot these red flag situations.

4. Should married couples have separate bank accounts or a joint account?

Approximately 50 percent of marriages end in divorce, and most of the cases cite financial problems as the root cause. Considering this, the issue of money—who has it, where it goes, who has access, and so on—should be discussed and discussed and discussed before the vows are made and the cake is cut.

It ultimately comes down to the specific individuals involved, but a good idea is for each person to maintain an individual account and have a joint account as well for monthly expenses such as food and bills. If both partners work, their contributions to the joint account should be based on a fair percentage of their wage. You get these percentages by dividing each individual's income by the couple's total income.

In money, like in marriage, there should be no secrets, no pride, and no low interest rates! To make your marriage and money last, keep communication open about your financial situation and discuss any and all large purchases.

5. I noticed a bank error on my statement in my favor. Do I get to keep the money?

Though it may seem like a gift from a higher power that you received this money, it is *not* yours and you are not entitled to it. Chances are the bank will discover the error and take it back.

If you have spent this money, you are liable to pay it back, and if you neglect to do so your credit will suffer—not to mention if the money is taken out after you have spent it, it could leave your account in the negative zone and you will be responsible for the overdraft charges. If you explain the mistake and return the money, you will feel good about being honest and maybe even receive a small gift of appreciation from the bank.

6. Can I get my overdraft fees waived?

It is possible to get your overdraft fees waived by your bank, but you are lucky if this happens. The key is to make them feel sorry for you, which shouldn't be a problem if the overdraft really wasn't your fault.

Let's say your employer was late depositing your paycheck and your rent was paid that day. Go to your bank and sit down with an account representative, explain to her that you know it is your fault about the fees, but say you were shocked at the overdraft rates.

The bank has every right to charge you, so ask them if there is anything you can do to avoid or at least reduce the charges. Add how loyal and responsible a customer you've been (assuming you *have* been) and that you would like to continue to be such a customer.

Afterward, send them a nice letter praising them. Again, the bank wants you as a customer, so they just might help you out, but do not go in the bank angry, expecting to have people bend over backward to help you.

NOTES:

REAL ESTATE
Making Sense Out of Property

Property ownership is big business. Whether you're buying, selling, renting, or flipping, your home can provide the security you need beyond lock and key.

Real estate runs a different track from other financial ventures because it's a market that most people are involved with one way or the other. If you're smart in your real estate choices and aware of what's going on, you could end up richer than you ever thought possible.

Keep in mind, though, that the real estate market is very much reliant on where you are living, so independent research is always necessary.

1. Real estate is a safe investment, isn't it?

Safe is a complicated word when it comes to investments. The real estate market is so dependent on the national economy and so many other variables that it can fluctuate up or down.

Generally, you will not pay the full price of your real estate investment but a fraction of it. Any growth the investment may see would apply to that initial principal. This way you can pay, say $15,000 for a $150,000 house and any rate increases on that investment will be taken off the $15,000. So even if the house value goes up 3 or 4 percent, it still may be a significant return on your small investment.

For short-term profit, invest in something other than real estate because you have to worry about property maintenance and this can be costly. This being said, real estate is also a good investment in that it opens up doors that were previously closed to you. If you own your own home, you are more easily approved for credit and obviously pay a mortgage rather than rent, which is a steadier payment.

2. Is it profitable to sublet your home?

Subletting can be a lucrative move, if you are able to pull it off and are willing to put up with the consequences.

First, you should be sure that you are allowed to sublet. (Some landlords prefer you not to.) Also, be careful of how much you will charge. There can be legal ramifications to asking for more rent than you actually pay. Find a lawyer who specializes in real estate to help you with the legal side of things.

On the plus side, subletting your home can be profitable when you will live outside the area for an extended period of time. Just make sure the tenant you sublet to is dependable.

As well, avoid setting up an illegal basement suite. Though these are everywhere in large cities, you can get into some big trouble if the property isn't zoned for it and if you are found out.

3. What is house flipping? How much money can you make?

House flipping is the process of buying a piece of real estate at a relatively low cost, improving the quality of the property, and selling it at a heightened cost in a quick amount of time. Necessary for the process to work is an interested investor, a talented and ambitious home renovator (or team of renovators), and the determination to carry it through.

Many investors use family and friends as renovators. There is definitely the potential to make a lot of money in a short amount of time, but there are consequences. Sometimes work is done too fast and the quality of the work suffers. That is why usually more than one appraisal on the house should be done before selling.

Many people make full-time careers out of house flipping and dedicate hundreds of hours of remodelling to realize a profit on their investment. There is no guarantee, however, that the price you sell the property for will match or exceed the money you put into fixing it up.

4. What are the benefits of owning a home over renting?

Most people dream of owning a home, and with this dream come benefits when compared to those who rent. As the value of the house rises over time, owners build equity and enjoy shrinking mortgage balances. Also, owners do not have to worry about housing costs skyrocketing because unless borrowers have adjustable-rate mortgages, lenders cannot increase rates and payments.

As a renter, your payments may increase many times without your consent. By owning a home, you are investing in more than just real estate; you are investing in your future. So be smart and plan ahead!

5. What are the downsides to owning rather than renting?

With ownership comes responsibility and lots of it! There is no landlord to complain to when the pipes break or when the furnace is shot. It's all up to you to fix.

This is why it's usually not a good idea to throw all your money into a huge down-payment, because you'll need a little extra cash in case something happens.

It is also very important that buyers understand where they stand in terms of job security. You do not want to be a new homeowner and newly unemployed! Payments can also add up unexpectedly and must be kept in mind. Buyers are often required to pay closing costs and other home-buying fees, along with a commission to the real estate agent.

As a renter, move-in costs are cheaper, usually a damage deposit and a security deposit, which may or may not be returned to you when you move out.

6. What should my monthly mortgage payment be in relation to my monthly net income?

Lenders and banks vary in their calculations for what is acceptable. Some lenders want your total ratio to be less than 36 percent for your home and 45 percent of your total debt. Some, however, allow up to 80 percent debt-to-income ratio to approve a mortgage loan.

It all depends on your situation and the willingness of your mortgage broker to give you a loan. Keep in mind that these payments can be refinanced later (fixed to adjustable rates) to accommodate changing financial circumstances.

7. What is better: a home equity loan or a second mortgage?

Really this depends on what you intend to do. A home equity loan is basically a line of credit and can be paid whenever you like. Most of the time there are no closing costs.

A second mortgage is a second lien on your house and issued as a one-time, lump-sum amount that can be borrowed on either a fixed or variable rate of interest.

Home equity loans have more flexibility and typically cost less, but a second mortgage may help if you only need to borrow money for one occasion, say to pay for a large investment. Just like any other loan, factors you should consider would be your income and risk tolerance.

8. How do I find out the value of my home? Is it important to know even if I'm not selling my home?

To know the value of your home is to know how much leverage you have in the financial world. To a creditor, a wink and a smile will only get you so far, whereas equity will get you much further.

It is important to know the value of your estate because many business loans and other kinds of loans are secured against real estate, meaning that agencies will lend you money only if you own property. (This protects them from refusal or lack of repayment.)

The best way to assess the value of your home is to hire a certified appraiser. Usually the homeowner is responsible for this payment, but many times residential appraisers agree to accept orders from lending institutions with the understanding that payment will be made following settlement or closing of the loan.

9. What do I do when looking for a real estate agent?

Searching for a real estate agent can be tricky business, but if you know what to look for, you could be saving yourself from trouble.

In any industry, experience is almost always an asset, but it is of particular importance in the real estate industry. Ask your agent how many sales they close a year, how many years they've conducted business, and what kind of training was necessary. You have a right to know this, and if your agent is a professional, he or she should have no problem answering your questions.

Further, there is no replacing good ol' skill. You need to know your agent can perform his or her duties confidently and wisely. Does your agent have intimate awareness of technical aspects of contracts such as negotiations, inspections, and appraisals?

Most real estate agents have market knowledge of a specific area in which they generally operate their business. An agent who specializes in the west end of the city may not be helpful when selling on the east end. By knowing the community in which you are buying or selling, the agent will be aware of comparable prices and what has happened, what is currently happening, and what is going to happen in the area.

Keep in mind that your agent works for you. The agent must have a proper work ethic and make an effort to work around your schedule, which includes evenings and weekends, to show your home. (This is when most buyers and sellers are available.)

Agents should always be easy to contact and not bogged down with other business. Remember, you are the priority!

Find an agent with integrity. You cannot put a price on honesty. Buying or selling your home is too big of a deal to have a sleaze as an agent, so make sure he or she is looking out for your best interests and not just looking to make a quick buck.

Lastly, resources are valuable assets in the business of real estate. Agents may have convenient website access to home listings and good relationships with mortgage brokers that could help you out. Any resource can be an advantage and will make you a buck or two!

---

10. How can I estimate moving costs?

Moving your belongings from your house can be a stressful and expensive chore. But unless you want to give up all of your possessions, it's pretty much necessary.

Plan ahead in order to get an idea of how much you're willing to spend. If you are using a moving company, call ahead and talk to a representative. Let them know the square footage of your home as well as any large pieces of furniture you own, and ask about any and all costs that are involved in the move. They should be able to give a rough estimate based on the number of boxes and materials needed. There is also typically a price chart available showing the distance the moving vehicle must travel and associated costs.

If you decide to move on your own, decide what size truck you need, or better yet, get a friend who owns a truck. (If you don't have a friend, GET ONE!)

Also consider what materials you will need (boxes, tape, etc.) and whether you'll need to hire additional help to move sensitive furniture or clean your home once it's empty. Establishing a moving budget prior to packing may open up room to reduce costs, but more importantly it will make a normally stressful day a little less stressful!

STOCK/ INVESTMENTS
Spread the Wealth

Benjamin Franklin once said, "An investment in knowledge always pays the best interest." Well, old Ben certainly knew what he was talking about.

The trick to investing properly (and profitably) is in understanding the market and making reasonable choices based on your risk tolerance. That may sound easy enough, but it's usually in the details where most people get lost.

There is a lot of money to be made in the stock market, so it's important that you understand just how much money you can make *and potentially lose* while playing the investment game.

1. What is stock in a company?

Stock is an investment in a company that sells shares of that company in order to raise money for expansion and improvements, and of course, for financial gain.

When you own stock, you are shareholder and own a part (or share) of the company. Each share of that stock is worth a certain price, which changes depending on how successful the company is (or often how successful it is *perceived* to be).

If you buy stock at ten dollars a share, and a year later the company has grown and an individual share is worth twenty dollars, you are doing very well. If a share is now worth five, well…you're not. (Until you sell the stock, the value is only on paper—the *realized* value, a gain or loss, is based on the selling price of a share on the day you sell it.)

Investing in stocks offers no guarantees, so be careful when choosing which stocks to buy. You can buy shares in a private company or a publicly traded company that is listed on a stock exchange such as the Dow Jones Industrial Average (DJIA). Typically you must be an accredited investor if you are interested in a private company, which means you represent a bank or a trust, are a director or executive, or are worth a lot of money.

2. I want to invest my money in something. What do I look for before I start?

Investments can be a daunting and intimidating task, especially if you've never invested before.

Make sure you are in a financially smart position before you begin; you do not want to be nose-deep in credit card debt or living paycheck to paycheck while throwing money into stock.

Next consider your choices of long-term investments. Consider your goals when doing this (child's education, retirement, etc.). This will give you a better understanding of the amount of time the investment will have to grow.

Choosing an investment is a tricky process, so meet with an investment broker whom you are sure has your best interests in mind. Some do not work with new or small accounts.

Spread your investments around to reduce risk. If stocks are low in value, bonds may be high. If you are a beginner investor, try mutual funds. They are usually low risk and diversify your portfolio.

Whatever you invest in, make sure you fully understand the ins and outs of the process. You will inevitably be more successful as an investor if you feel confident in the people you are investing in. Make sure you understand the short- and long-term goals of the company and whether it can be successful in its business. This takes education and guesswork, so tread carefully.

---

3. My good friend told me to invest in something I've never heard of. But he swears it is a guarantee. Should I invest?

It's your money, so only invest in something you are comfortable with . The market is dependent on so many variables that NOTHING IS A GUARANTEE.

If, after doing some research, you feel the management of the company can succeed in both slow and fast times, then invest. Especially when dealing with smaller companies, it always comes down to the person you're investing in. You can have a great idea and the person in charge can ruin it, whereas a good leader can make a success out of anything.

No matter what, focus on what's on paper and what your gut says, not on what somebody else is telling you.

4. Is there any way to predict how the stock market will shift?

The best way to "predict the future" and make money is to buy shares at a very low price, private placements for example, and sell high when the company goes IPO (goes public). This is how you make real cash.

If you are curious about what factors drive certain sectors of the stock market, there are several books and articles on stock market theory.

Mainly you have to look at the macroeconomics. This includes government decisions, international factors, and entry and exit of well-known investors into certain sectors. The U.S. stock market contains corporations that account for about 60 percent of the world's economy, which makes the New York Stock Exchange (NYSE) a major influence.

An easy way (using the term loosely) to research a sector is by accessing a firm's securities research. Otherwise you can access governmental statistics Web sites such as the Federal Reserve Board.

Whatever you do, remember that the stock market will always be unpredictable. Anything that affects how people spend money ultimately affects the stock market, so play with caution.

5. Are there ways to safely practice investing in the stockmarket?

A fun way to gain necessary market knowledge is to access a website that offers a simulation of the stock market, giving you play money, with which you can practice for free.

This is not only a safe way to get to know the market for those who have no clue how it works; it also can be fun to invest tons of money that you don't have just to see what happens.

The site also can assist sophisticated investors looking to test out advanced strategies. These sites have a system that connects to a real-life data feed and can support trading in North American exchanges, option trading, and short selling, and adjusts for most corporate actions such as mergers and dividends. So get online, have fun, and become a virtual millionaire (or a virtual bum)!

6. How do I begin to "play" in the stock market?

Before investing your hard-earned dollars, a key recommendation would be to educate yourself about the market.

Knowledge will get you much further than luck when it comes to the stock market. Many factors determine where people invest their money: news reports, world events, astrology, because the dog barked at the TV when a stock appeared, etc.

How you invest is ultimately up to you, but to begin effectively, learn how the best traders are buying and selling and why. You can do this on the stock simulator on free websites, or do your own research with top traders that you know, in person or in books.

In case these top traders are tight-lipped in terms of their investments (You can't blame them.), you can always model your trading on somebody who is very successful. Of course, there are no guarantees, but it might give you a better idea of how the game is played. Nothing beats experience, so either imitate somebody else's or get your own.

7. What should I look for in insurance companies?

Do not put your life in the wrong hands!

When shopping for any kind of insurance, you should always consider the firm's financial condition. It is important that the company you choose can and will pay your claim.

Secondly, you need to have a good knowledge of your insurance needs. This will depend on your specific situation.

Lastly, it will serve you well to shop around for the best rate for what you need. An easy way to do this would be surfing the web (some websites provide price comparisons) or by calling companies and asking for rate information.

8. What is the difference between registered and non-registered funds?

Registered funds protect your investments and their earnings from tax, whereas unregistered funds do not.

Typically, a registered fund is used for long-term investments, such as a child's education or retirement. A non-registered fund may be more fitting for short- term investments, like saving for a car or a vacation.

9. What are the advantages and disadvantages to mutual funds?

This is like asking how many raindrops are in a cloud. The sector exploded in the 1990s, and now there are currently over 80 million Americans that invest in mutual funds.

A mutual fund is a company that raises money by selling shares to its investors. In return for purchasing shares, investors receive a proportional share in the pool of fund assets.

There is a range in degrees of diversification between mutual funds. Generally, one advantage to a mutual fund investment is that it gives small investors access to a well-diversified portfolio of securities such as equities and bonds.

Another advantage to mutual funds is liquidity. Shares can be bought and sold by the shareholder and can be accessed whenever necessary.

Mutual fund investments typically fail to beat the market, however, and it is difficult to pick a fund that has a better chance to do well. That is to say, past performance has little influence on future standings. When selling your mutual fund, be aware of tax consequences and back-end loads (charges that affect your total redemption value).

A fund manager invests your money based on market conditions in order to reach specified objectives that are in the original prospectus. Deciding which mutual fund to invest in and with what company is up to you, but due diligence will certainly serve you well in this case.

IDENTITY THEFT

Signposts to Watch for on the Information Highway

In this fast-paced world of technology, e-commerce is definitely here to stay and has become a simple, quick, and convenient way to check your accounts, transfer funds, pay bills, and track transactions. The luxury of having your personal information available to you at a moment's notice certainly beats standing in line at the bank. However, with every good invention come those who want to exploit it. As a responsible online user, you must be aware and proceed cautiously to effectively protect your personal business. Being a victim of identity theft can be a costly problem, both in time and expense. Victims spend time fixing their credit reports and closing bad accounts while establishing new ones, and it becomes more difficult to obtain a loan and even a job.

1. What are the dangers of online banking?

Online banking can be a fairly safe practice as long as you are careful of what you are doing and stay updated on scams and dangers. Banking sites utilize encryption software, which makes your information inaccessible until it is "unlocked," or decrypted.

Always be cautious of how much information you give on-line. Personal information that you assume to be safe through certain corporations can be sold to data brokers who will use it for database filing. Make sure the site you are using has guarantees against this.

Be aware! Banking sites *never* send out unsolicited emails requesting personal information! E-mails like these mimic real, professional sites and, unless you are careful, can access important information about you or manipulate settings such as IP addresses and computer settings.

Do not open these e-mails!

2. How can I reduce the risk of online identity theft?

E-mail, unlike banking sites, is not usually encrypted, so never send mail with account numbers, credit card numbers, or any other personal information.

Always sign out of online accounts. Logging out once you are leaving a web site is like locking the door (your password being the key).

In addition, when discarding computers, do it safely. Destroy any discs, CDs, or DVDs that may have personal information on them.

When replacing your computer system, delete all information on your hard drive. Keep in mind that deleting a file is not enough! It can still be accessed, so be sure to use a "white-space wiper" program to make access to these "deleted" files impossible.

Finally, remember to carefully review your credit card statements each month for unauthorized purchases or charges made on your behalf. If you notice some suspicious activity, contact your bank or credit card company immediately.

If you still feel uncomfortable using your credit card online or performing any financial transactions, here are some ways to protect yourself. Always make sure your browser is the latest, most updated version. This takes advantage of any encryption capabilities.

In addition to this, install a firewall and have updated spyware software installed in your computer. Look for a padlock

symbol in the upper or lower corner of web pages you are on; this icon indicates that the page is secure.

Also, look for an S after the usual http:/ URL (https:/). This also indicates a secure server.

3. How can I reduce the risk of becoming a victim of other kinds of identity theft?

Though you cannot eliminate the risk completely, there are steps you can take to reduce the risk of identity theft.

Always keep updated identification documents in a safe place. This includes photocopies of all cards inside your wallet or purse. This will not protect you from fraud but will save you a headache if anything happens to the information.

Know whom you are giving information to. This means verifying the identity of the person requesting your information, especially if they contacted you.

Destroy personal information when you no longer need it. (Identity thieves are garbage-pickers!) This includes all account statements, old identification cards, and loan applications.

A paper shredder may be a wise investment for your home. Keep any financial information that you don't regularly need on your person at home. Not only will losing this information increase your chances of identity theft, it will cost you time and money to replace these documents.

If you note anything is lost or stolen, report it immediately! Reporting the loss of debit or credit cards reduces the risk of others using them and racking up your account balances.

For extra insurance, limit personal information on a check. Have your initials printed on your checks and never write down the complete account number.

And finally, always protect your passwords! Shield keypads when entering passwords in public. Choose passwords that are difficult to guess, and change them regularly.

A
BUILDING
WEALTH
CHALLENGE

Getting Yourself
into Financial Shape

START NOW

I have a personal challenge for you.

These few steps are hard to take—they require some dedication to turning your finances around, but can immediately begin to cut your spending, cut your expenses, and increase your savings.

Are you ready to try?

1. Go get your pay stub, or calculate how much money on average you net a month. (net = take home after taxes)

2. Collect ALL of your credit cards, debit cards, and any other department store cards you may have. Getting scared? I hope so!

3. Now, go to your drawer and pull out your scissors. Prepare yourself, but don't do anything yet.

4. Now what I need you to do is THINK about all those little five dollar purchases you make with your debit card, THINK about all of the ATM fees you have paid the bank. Pick up your debit card. Pick up your scissors. And yes, cut the debit card to bits.

With your debit card gone, you will lose the convenience of easy cash withdrawals at any time of the day or night. But you can save yourself potentially hundreds of dollars a week.

Once a week, go to the teller at you local bank branch and ask to withdraw $50.00 cash—no more, no less. I promise that the next time you want to buy a three-dollar coffee and you have to go to the bank teller because you have spent your weekly fifty dollars, you will begin to take note of your true spending habits. (I just saved you three dollars for the coffee, and a two dollar charge for the ATM transaction fee. If you save this $5 only once a week it still adds up to a savings of:

$5 a week x 52 weeks a year = $260 annual savings.

Let's keep going with the experiment:

1. Gather all your credit and retail credit cards.

2. Calculate how much your take home pay is (NET PAY, what can you *really* afford to spend?)

3. Look at the cash back or points program of your current credit card. Look at the interest rates of each card. Find one with a 30 day no-interest grace period. The card that has the lowest interest rate, best points program, and a grace period is the ONE card you will keep.

4. Cut up all the other cards.

5. Pay off the remaining balances on the cards you have destroyed until you are only receiving one credit card bill a month.

6. When you have paid off the now-destroyed cards, call up the credit card company and ask that they lower your remaining card's credit limit to equal:

Your take home pay $ 5000.00

Minus your necessary monthly payments, e.g. mortgage + car + utilities ($1000.00 + $ 300.00 + $500.00) = $ 1800.00

NEW CREDIT CARD LIMIT = $ 3,200.00

7. Now, when you make a purchase use only your ONE major credit card.

8. At the end of each month break down your costs (i.e.: housing, transportation, food, entertainment, savings, general maintenance). If you do the cost analysis for at least six months, you will have an accurate idea of where you spend your money, and where it would be easiest to cut spending. (see chart below)

MONTHLY EXPENDITURES

	Mo 1	Mo 2	Mo 3	Mo 4	Mo 5	Mo 6	AVG
HOUSING							
TRASPORTATION							
FOOD							
SAVINGS							
ENTERTAINMENT							

(feel free to add more rows in order to accurately reflect your lifestyle)

When your general budget is done for the total expenditures add up all of your bills for six months. After the six months, add up all your totals from left to right then divide by 6 (month 1+2+3+4+5+6 / 6 = average monthly spending)

At the end of six months you will have an accurate picture of your spending habits. Now instead of paying ATM fees and high interest on your purchases you get cash back or rewards points. Instead of the credit card company charging you for the use of their card, you are paying off your bills interest-free and reaping the benefits.

FOR FURTHER REVIEW:

At the end of the six month term, after you have your average expenditure for each group, take it to the next level. Break your budget down further to save even more money!

A basic budget should look like the chart below, but make sure to customize it to fit your specific needs. For instance, the housing category may need additional sub-categories if you are renovating your home or adding a pool. (see chart below)

EXPENDITURE BREAKDOWN

Allocation 100%	Mo 1	Mo 2	Mo 3	Mo 4	Mo 5	Mo 6	AVG
HOUSING							
Mortgage							
Utilities							
Add sub-categories as needed							
TRANSPORTATION							
Payments on Car							
Insurance							
Gasoline							
FOOD							
SAVINGS							
Vacation							
Retirement							
Education Fund							
Emergency Fund							
ENTERTAINMENT							

After you have spent six months discovering what you spend, use the chart to delve even further into your spending habits: figure out exactly where you are spending your money. Remember, without this education you can not ensure that you are making the right spending choices. Use this diagram to keep repeating the steps, making a new budget every six months to a year as economic conditions change.

The chart will also show you how to divide your income into percentages. Knowing your spending percentages helps you to reallocate your resources. For instance, knowing that you spend $600 on entertainment may not seem significant. Knowing that the $600 is 40% of your pay puts it into perspective.

The sample budget below assumes your take home pay is $3000.00 a month ($36,000 per year) for a single person household. If you are married with one child, the chart remains the same; if you are a single parent with child, decrease the entertainment allocation by 5% and add it to the food allocation. This would be a fantastic budget that will allow you to do all the things you want, without sacrifice.

Allocation 100% Single person.	Percentage of Income	$ as per monthly wage
HOUSING	40%	$1200.00
TRANSPORTATION	15%	$450.00
FOOD	10%	$300.00
SAVINGS	25%	$750.00
ENTERTAINMENT	10%	$300.00

A FINAL NOTE

I strongly believe that if you execute these actions in your everyday life, lower expenses where necessary, and always ask yourself *why* you spend the way you do, you will succeed in achieving financial fitness.

The goal is not to deprive yourself. It is to fully understand the cost of your spending habits. If you want to buy a $100 shirt you should ask yourself, "How long will I have to work to pay for it?" If you work at a $10 an hour job, and the shirt costs $100, do the math: $100 shirt/ $10 an hour wage = 10 hours of work. Is it worth it?

If you follow these simple steps and use the answers provided in this book, you will see positive results right away. Financial fitness is a life journey that must be maintained.

If you continue to practice what you have learned in this book, you will learn how to live your life debt-free while still enjoying all the things that you most love.

Here's to your success!

NOTES:

NOTES: